OLIVIA
RODRIGO
QUIZ BOOK

INTRODUCTION

Compiled in this book are over 100 questions on everything Olivia Rodrigo.

Topics include; her personal life, music career, albums, singles, tours and more!

The difficulty of the questions vary so any Olivia Rodrigo fan should be able to enjoy and be challenged by the quizzes.

So let's start testing your super fan knowledge on all things Olivia Rodrigo!

1. When was Olivia Rodrigo born?

2. Where was Olivia Rodrigo born?

3. What are the names of Olivia Rodrigo's parents?

4. What is Olivia Rodrigo's middle name?

5. What is Olivia Rodrigo's ethnic background?

6. What condition was Olivia Rodrigo born with in her left ear?

7. **Which elementary school did Olivia Rodrigo attend?**

8. **At what age did Olivia Rodrigo start taking vocal lessons?**

9. **What was the name of Olivia Rodrigo's first "proper song" that she posted on Instagram?**

10. **Which Disney Channel series did Olivia Rodrigo star in before "High School Musical: The Musical: The Series"?**

11. **Who was Olivia Rodrigo's co-star and rumored boyfriend from "High School Musical: The Musical: The Series"?**

12. **Which actor did Olivia Rodrigo date in 2018?**

13. **What hobby does Olivia Rodrigo enjoy in her free time?**

14. **What is Olivia Rodrigo's favorite book series?**

15. **What type of music did Olivia Rodrigo grow up listening to, influenced by her parents?**

16. **Which famous pop star inspired Olivia Rodrigo to start songwriting?**

17. What instrument did Olivia Rodrigo learn to play for her role in "Bizaardvark"?

18. What is Olivia Rodrigo's favorite holiday?

19. Which family tradition does Olivia Rodrigo's family follow due to their Filipino heritage?

20. What was Olivia Rodrigo's first acting role?

21. Which song by Olivia Rodrigo became a breakout hit in early 2021?

22. What is the title of Olivia Rodrigo's debut album released in May 2021?

23. Which track from the album "SOUR" is said to be a continuation of "drivers license"?

24. In the song "good 4 u", what insult does Olivia use in the final chorus?

25. Olivia Rodrigo co-starred in which Disney+ TV series?

26. Which social media platform does Olivia use to promote snippets of her songs before they're released?

27. How many tracks are there on the "SOUR" album?

28. Which "SOUR" song starts with the lyrics, "Know that I loved you so bad"?

29. What is Olivia Rodrigo's middle name?

30. Which song from "SOUR" includes the lyrics "Don't you think I loved you too much to be used and discarded"?

31. How old was Olivia when she wrote her first song?

32. Which "SOUR" song mentions Billy Joel?

33. What musical instrument does Olivia often play during her performances?

34. Which famous pop-punk band's sound inspired some tracks of "SOUR"?

35. How many weeks did "drivers license" stay at No. 1 on the Billboard Hot 100?

36. Olivia was nominated for seven of which major award in 2022?

37. What is the opening track of the "SOUR" album?

38. Which song from "SOUR" includes the lyrics "I got my driver's license last week"?

39. What is the name of Olivia Rodrigo's second studio album released in 2023?

40. **Which song from "GUTS" features the lyrics "I hate to give the satisfaction, asking how you're doing now"?**

41. **Olivia Rodrigo won her first Grammy Award in which year?**

42. **Which song did Olivia Rodrigo perform at the 2022 Grammy Awards?**

43. **What is the name of the character Olivia Rodrigo plays in "High School Musical: The Musical: The Series"?**

44. Which song from "SOUR" talks about feeling insecure due to social media comparisons?

45. Olivia Rodrigo collaborated with which artist on the song "1 step forward, 3 steps back"?

46. Which song from "GUTS" includes the lyrics "I know their beauty's not my lack"?

47. What is the name of Olivia Rodrigo's debut single?

48. Which song from "SOUR" includes the lyrics "I hope you're happy, but not like how you were with me"?

49. Olivia Rodrigo's song "traitor" is about what theme?

50. Which song from "GUTS" features the lyrics "Look at you, cool guy, you got it"?

51. What is the name of the song Olivia Rodrigo wrote for the Disney+ series "High School Musical: The Musical: The Series"?

52. Which song from "SOUR" includes the lyrics "I wore makeup when we dated"?

53. Olivia Rodrigo's song "brutal" addresses what theme?

54. What is the name of Olivia Rodrigo's second single released in 2021?

55. What is the name of Olivia Rodrigo's nonprofit organization?

56. Which organization does Olivia Rodrigo partner with for her U.S. tour to support reproductive healthcare?

57. **What was the purpose of Olivia Rodrigo's special one-night-only concert event in Los Angeles?**

58. **What initiative did Olivia Rodrigo support by designing and selling a T-shirt called "Spicy Pisces"?**

59. **How many Grammy Awards has Olivia Rodrigo won?**

60. **Which award did Olivia Rodrigo win for her song "drivers license" at the 2021 MTV Video Music Awards?**

61. **In which year did Olivia Rodrigo win the Billboard Music Award for Top New Artist?**

62. **Which prestigious title did Time magazine award Olivia Rodrigo in 2021?**

63. **How many Billboard Music Awards has Olivia Rodrigo won?**

64. **Which award did Olivia Rodrigo win at the 2022 Brit Awards?**

65. **What honor did Olivia Rodrigo receive from Billboard in 2022?**

66. **Which song earned Olivia Rodrigo the iHeartRadio Music Award for Best New Pop Artist in 2022?**

67. How many MTV Video Music Awards has Olivia Rodrigo won?

68. Which award did Olivia Rodrigo win at the 2022 American Music Awards?

69. Who was Paige Olvera's best friend and co-star on "Bizaardvark"?

70. What is the main premise of "Bizaardvark"?

71. What musical instrument does Paige Olvera play on "Bizaardvark"?

72. In which year did Olivia Rodrigo start her role as Paige Olvera on "Bizaardvark"?

73. How many seasons did "Bizaardvark" run?

74. What is the name of the studio where Paige and Frankie film their videos in "Bizaardvark"?

75. What is the name of the song Paige and Frankie perform in the first episode of "Bizaardvark"?

76. What is the main theme of the videos created by Paige and Frankie on "Bizaardvark"?

77. In which season of "High School Musical: The Musical: The Series" does Olivia Rodrigo's character, Nini, play Gabriella Montez in the school musical?

78. Who is Nini's love interest in "High School Musical: The Musical: The Series"?

79. What song did Olivia Rodrigo's character, Nini, write and perform in Season 2 that went viral?

80. Why did Olivia Rodrigo's character, Nini, leave East High in Season 2?

81. What is the name of the school where "High School Musical: The Musical: The Series" is set?

82. In which season did Olivia Rodrigo's role as Nini become a recurring character rather than a main character?

83. What is the name of the musical production that Nini and her friends put on in Season 1?

84. Which song did Olivia Rodrigo's character, Nini, sing as her audition piece for the school musical in Season 1?

85. Why did Olivia Rodrigo decide to reduce her role in "High School Musical: The Musical: The Series"?

86. What is the name of Olivia Rodrigo's 2024-2025 world tour?

87. When does Olivia Rodrigo's GUTS World Tour kick off?

88. **Which city will host the opening concert of Olivia Rodrigo's GUTS World Tour?**

89. **How many dates are scheduled for Olivia Rodrigo's GUTS World Tour?**

90. **Which venues in London will Olivia Rodrigo perform at during her GUTS World Tour?**

91. **What is the final city and venue for Olivia Rodrigo's GUTS World Tour?**

92. **Which European cities are included in Olivia Rodrigo's GUTS World Tour?**

93. What special item is available for purchase as part of Olivia Rodrigo's GUTS World Tour merchandise?

94. Which song is Olivia Rodrigo known to perform as part of her setlist on the GUTS World Tour?

95. Which organization is Olivia Rodrigo partnering with for her U.S. tour to support reproductive healthcare?

96. Who was Olivia Rodrigo's co-star and rumored boyfriend from "High School Musical: The Musical: The Series"?

97. **Which Disney Channel star did Olivia Rodrigo date in 2018?**

98. **Who did Olivia Rodrigo date after her breakup with producer Adam Faze?**

99. **Which actor was Olivia Rodrigo rumored to be dating in late 2023?**

100. **What inspired many of the songs on Olivia Rodrigo's debut album "SOUR"?**

Sour Track List

Can you complete the track list in order?

(Answers in the back)

1. _____

2. _____

3. _____

4. _____

5. _____

6. _____

7. _____

8. _____

9. _____

10. _____

11. _____

Guts Track List

Can you complete the track list in order?

(Answers in the back)

1. _____

2. _____

3. _____

4. _____

5. _____

6. _____

7. _____

8. _____

9. _____

10. _____

11. _____

12. _____

ANSWERS

How did you do?

0-20 Correct Answers
You're just becoming a fan.

21-40 Correct Answers
You're a casual fan.

41-60 Correct Answers
You're a big fan.

61-80 Correct Answers
You're a huge fan.

81-100 Correct Answers
You're an Olivia Rodrigo Superfan!

1. **When was Olivia Rodrigo born?**
   - February 20, 2003
2. **Where was Olivia Rodrigo born?**
   - Murrieta, California
3. **What are the names of Olivia Rodrigo's parents?**
   - Jennifer and Chris Rodrigo
4. **What is Olivia Rodrigo's middle name?**
   - Isabel
5. **What is Olivia Rodrigo's ethnic background?**
   - Filipino, German, and Irish
6. **What condition was Olivia Rodrigo born with in her left ear?**
   - She was born half-deaf in her left ear.
7. **Which elementary school did Olivia Rodrigo attend?**
   - Lisa J. Mails Elementary School

8. **At what age did Olivia Rodrigo start taking vocal lessons?**
   - ○ At age 5
9. **What was the name of Olivia Rodrigo's first "proper song" that she posted on Instagram?**
   - ○ "Naive Girl"
10. **Which Disney Channel series did Olivia Rodrigo star in before "High School Musical: The Musical: The Series"?**
    - ○ "Bizaardvark"
11. **Who was Olivia Rodrigo's co-star and rumored boyfriend from "High School Musical: The Musical: The Series"?**
    - ○ Joshua Bassett
12. **Which actor did Olivia Rodrigo date in 2018?**
    - ○ Ethan Wacker
13. **What hobby does Olivia Rodrigo enjoy in her free time?**
    - ○ Knitting

14. **What is Olivia Rodrigo's favorite book series?**
   - Harry Potter
15. **What type of music did Olivia Rodrigo grow up listening to, influenced by her parents?**
   - Alternative rock
16. **Which famous pop star inspired Olivia Rodrigo to start songwriting?**
   - Taylor Swift
17. **What instrument did Olivia Rodrigo learn to play for her role in "Bizaardvark"?**
   - Guitar
18. **What is Olivia Rodrigo's favorite holiday?**
   - Christmas
19. **Which family tradition does Olivia Rodrigo's family follow due to their Filipino heritage?**
   - Filipino cuisine and traditions

20. **What was Olivia Rodrigo's first acting role?**
- Paige Olvera in "Bizaardvark"

21. **Which song by Olivia Rodrigo became a breakout hit in early 2021?**

- **"drivers license"**

22. **What is the title of Olivia Rodrigo's debut album released in May 2021?**

- **"SOUR"**

23. **Which track from the album "SOUR" is said to be a continuation of "drivers license"?**

- **"deja vu"**

24. In the song "good 4 u", what insult does Olivia use in the final chorus?

   ○ "sociopath"

25. Olivia Rodrigo co-starred in which Disney+ TV series?

   ○ "High School Musical: The Musical: The Series"

26. Which social media platform does Olivia use to promote snippets of her songs before they're released?

   ○ Instagram

27. How many tracks are there on the "SOUR" album?

   ○ 11 tracks

28. **Which "SOUR" song starts with the lyrics, "Know that I loved you so bad"?**

- o "favorite crime"

29. **What is Olivia Rodrigo's middle name?**

- o Isabel

30. **Which song from "SOUR" includes the lyrics "Don't you think I loved you too much to be used and discarded"?**

- o "enough for you"

31. **How old was Olivia when she wrote her first song?**

- o 5 years old

32. Which "SOUR" song mentions Billy Joel?

o "deja vu"

33. What musical instrument does Olivia often play during her performances?

o Piano

34. Which famous pop-punk band's sound inspired some tracks of "SOUR"?

o Paramore

35. How many weeks did "drivers license" stay at No. 1 on the Billboard Hot 100?

o 8 weeks

36.   Olivia was nominated for seven of which major award in 2022?

   o **Grammy Awards**

37.   What is the opening track of the "SOUR" album?

   o **"brutal"**

38.   Which song from "SOUR" includes the lyrics "I got my driver's license last week"?
   o "drivers license"

39.   What is the name of Olivia Rodrigo's second studio album released in 2023?
   o "GUTS"

40. **Which song from "GUTS" features the lyrics "I hate to give the satisfaction, asking how you're doing now"?**
   - ∘ "vampire"
41. **Olivia Rodrigo won her first Grammy Award in which year?**
   - ∘ 2022
42. **Which song did Olivia Rodrigo perform at the 2022 Grammy Awards?**
   - ∘ "drivers license"
43. **What is the name of the character Olivia Rodrigo plays in "High School Musical: The Musical: The Series"?**
   - ∘ Nini Salazar-Roberts
44. **Which song from "SOUR" talks about feeling insecure due to social media comparisons?**
   - ∘ "jealousy, jealousy"

45. **Olivia Rodrigo collaborated with which artist on the song "1 step forward, 3 steps back"?**
    - Taylor Swift (credited as a songwriter)
46. **Which song from "GUTS" includes the lyrics "I know their beauty's not my lack"?**
    - "jealousy, jealousy"
47. **What is the name of Olivia Rodrigo's debut single?**
    - "drivers license"
48. **Which song from "SOUR" includes the lyrics "I hope you're happy, but not like how you were with me"?**
    - "happier"
49. **Olivia Rodrigo's song "traitor" is about what theme?**
    - Betrayal in a relationship

50. **Which song from "GUTS" features the lyrics "Look at you, cool guy, you got it"?**
   - o "vampire"
51. **What is the name of the song Olivia Rodrigo wrote for the Disney+ series "High School Musical: The Musical: The Series"?**
   - o "All I Want"
52. **Which song from "SOUR" includes the lyrics "I wore makeup when we dated"?**
   - o "enough for you"
53. **Olivia Rodrigo's song "brutal" addresses what theme?**
   - o The pressures and struggles of teenage life
54. **What is the name of Olivia Rodrigo's second single released in 2021?**
   - o "deja vu"

55. **What is the name of Olivia Rodrigo's nonprofit organization?**
   - Fund 4 Good
56. **Which organization does Olivia Rodrigo partner with for her U.S. tour to support reproductive healthcare?**
   - National Network of Abortion Funds.
57. **What was the purpose of Olivia Rodrigo's special one-night-only concert event in Los Angeles?**
   - To raise money for her nonprofit, Fund 4 Good.
58. **What initiative did Olivia Rodrigo support by designing and selling a T-shirt called "Spicy Pisces"?**
   - She's the First (STF), through the Plus1 program.

59. **How many Grammy Awards has Olivia Rodrigo won?**
   ○ Three Grammy Awards
60. **Which award did Olivia Rodrigo win for her song "drivers license" at the 2021 MTV Video Music Awards?**
   ○ Song of the Year
61. **In which year did Olivia Rodrigo win the Billboard Music Award for Top New Artist?**
   ○ 2022
62. **Which prestigious title did Time magazine award Olivia Rodrigo in 2021?**
   ○ Entertainer of the Year
63. **How many Billboard Music Awards has Olivia Rodrigo won?**
   ○ Seven Billboard Music Awards

64. **Which award did Olivia Rodrigo win at the 2022 Brit Awards?**
   - International Song of the Year for "good 4 u"
65. **What honor did Olivia Rodrigo receive from Billboard in 2022?**
   - Woman of the Year
66. **Which song earned Olivia Rodrigo the iHeartRadio Music Award for Best New Pop Artist in 2022?**
   - "drivers license"
67. **How many MTV Video Music Awards has Olivia Rodrigo won?**
   - Four MTV Video Music Awards
68. **Which award did Olivia Rodrigo win at the 2022 American Music Awards?**
   - New Artist of the Year

69. **Who was Paige Olvera's best friend and co-star on "Bizaardvark"?**
   ○ Frankie Wong, played by Madison Hu
70. **What is the main premise of "Bizaardvark"?**
   ○ The show follows two best friends, Paige and Frankie, who create funny songs and videos for their online channel, Bizaardvark.
71. **What musical instrument does Paige Olvera play on "Bizaardvark"?**
   ○ Guitar
72. **In which year did Olivia Rodrigo start her role as Paige Olvera on "Bizaardvark"?**
   ○ 2016
73. **How many seasons did "Bizaardvark" run?**
   ○ Three seasons

74. **What is the name of the studio where Paige and Frankie film their videos in "Bizaardvark"?**
   ○ Vuuugle Studios
75. **What is the name of the song Paige and Frankie perform in the first episode of "Bizaardvark"?**
   ○ "The Comeback Song"
76. **What is the main theme of the videos created by Paige and Frankie on "Bizaardvark"?**
   ○ Comedy and music
77. **In which season of "High School Musical: The Musical: The Series" does Olivia Rodrigo's character, Nini, play Gabriella Montez in the school musical?**
   ○ Season 1

78. **Who is Nini's love interest in "High School Musical: The Musical: The Series"?**
   ○ Ricky Bowen, played by Joshua Bassett
79. **What song did Olivia Rodrigo's character, Nini, write and perform in Season 2 that went viral?**
   ○ "The Rose Song"
80. **Why did Olivia Rodrigo's character, Nini, leave East High in Season 2?**
   ○ To attend the Youth Actors Conservatory
81. **What is the name of the school where "High School Musical: The Musical: The Series" is set?**
   ○ East High School

82.   **In which season did Olivia Rodrigo's role as Nini become a recurring character rather than a main character?**
   o Season 3
83.   **What is the name of the musical production that Nini and her friends put on in Season 1?**
   o "High School Musical"
84.   **Which song did Olivia Rodrigo's character, Nini, sing as her audition piece for the school musical in Season 1?**
   o "Start of Something New"
85.   **Why did Olivia Rodrigo decide to reduce her role in "High School Musical: The Musical: The Series"?**
   o To focus on her music career, especially after the success of her debut single "drivers license"

86. **What is the name of Olivia Rodrigo's 2024-2025 world tour?**
   ○ GUTS World Tour
87. **When does Olivia Rodrigo's GUTS World Tour kick off?**
   ○ February 23, 2024
88. **Which city will host the opening concert of Olivia Rodrigo's GUTS World Tour?**
   ○ Palm Springs, California
89. **How many dates are scheduled for Olivia Rodrigo's GUTS World Tour?**
   ○ 57 dates
90. **Which venues in London will Olivia Rodrigo perform at during her GUTS World Tour?**
   ○ The O2 Arena

91. **What is the final city and venue for Olivia Rodrigo's GUTS World Tour?**
   ○ Los Angeles, California at the Kia Forum
92. **Which European cities are included in Olivia Rodrigo's GUTS World Tour?**
   ○ Amsterdam, Paris, and London, among others.
93. **What special item is available for purchase as part of Olivia Rodrigo's GUTS World Tour merchandise?**
   ○ GUTS World Tour beach towel.
94. **Which song is Olivia Rodrigo known to perform as part of her setlist on the GUTS World Tour?**
   ○ "drivers license" (among others)

95.   **Which organization is Olivia Rodrigo partnering with for her U.S. tour to support reproductive healthcare?**
   o National Network of Abortion Funds.
96.   **Who was Olivia Rodrigo's co-star and rumored boyfriend from "High School Musical: The Musical: The Series"?**
   o Joshua Bassett
97.   **Which Disney Channel star did Olivia Rodrigo date in 2018?**
   o Ethan Wacker
98.   **Who did Olivia Rodrigo date after her breakup with producer Adam Faze?**
   o Zack Bia

99. **Which actor was Olivia Rodrigo rumored to be dating in late 2023?**
   o Louis Partridge
100. **What inspired many of the songs on Olivia Rodrigo's debut album "SOUR"?**
   o Her breakup with Joshua Bassett

Sour Track List

Answers

1. Brutal
2. Traitor
3. Drivers License
4. 1 Step Forward, 3 Steps Back
5. Deja vu
6. Good 4 U
7. Enough For You
8. Happier
9. Jealousy, Jealousy
10. Favorite Crime
11. Hope Ur Ok

Guts (Standard Edition)
Track List

Answers

1. All-American Bitch
2. Bad Idea Right?
3. Vampire
4. Lacy
5. Ballad of a Homeschooled Girl
6. Making the Bed
7. Logical
8. Get Him Back!
9. Love is Embarrassing
10. The Grudge
11. Pretty Isn't Pretty
12. Teenage Dream

I really hope you enjoyed this book, tested your knowledge on all things Olivia Rodrigo and learnt new facts along the way!

If you would recommend this book, please consider leaving a review on Amazon!

Thank you

Made in the USA
Las Vegas, NV
29 November 2024

12880243R00036